E THE ELEPHANT
AND THE SCRUB FOREST

Text and photographs
Dave Taylor

Animals and their Ecosystems Series

Crabtree Publishing Company

A
Bobbie
Kalman
Book

Animals and Their Ecosystems Series
Dave Taylor

Editor-in-Chief
Bobbie Kalman

Editors
Christine Arthurs
Marni Hoogeveen
Janine Schaub

Design and pasteup
Adriana Longo

All photographs by Dave Taylor except the following:
World Wildlife Fund: p. 29 top and p. 31 top.

For Mom and Dad

I wish to thank the African Safari Club for its assistance in arranging the safari that took me to see these magnificent animals.

The people of Kenya have preserved part of the world's heritage. We owe them a debt of gratitude.

Cataloguing in Publication Data

Taylor, J. David, 1948-
      The elephant and the scrub forest

(Animals and their ecosystems)
Includes index.
ISBN 0-86505-365-0 (bound) ISBN 0-86505-395-2 (pbk.)

1. Elephants - Juvenile literature. 2. Elephants - Ecology - Juvenile literature. 3. Forest ecology - Juvenile literature. I. Title. II. Series.

QL737.P98T3 1990   j599.6'1

350 Fifth Ave	1110 Kamato Road	73 Lime Walk
Suite 3308	Unit 4	Headington
New York	Mississauga, Ontario	Oxford 0X3 7AD
NY 10118	Canada L4W 2P3	United Kingdom

Contents

The elephant and the scrub forest

Mama Tembo, an African elephant, stands quietly for a moment, holding up her giant ears to listen for distant sounds. Then she lowers her head and moves on. Her family follows behind, walking gracefully through the short, bushy trees of its favorite habitat, a scrub forest located in East Africa. Its members still live in the wild, free to roam from scrub forest to grassland to rain forest.

The scrub forest is home for a wide variety of wild animals including this herd of African elephants.

Most people are moved by their first encounter with elephants. These massive animals can give gentle caresses with their trunks or lethal stabs with their tusks. They are highly intelligent creatures that form complex animal societies. Elephants also have a great effect on their surroundings: they can destroy a forest or be the reason that a new one develops. To see these giant wonders of nature living free in the African wilderness is a remarkable experience.

Living in a changing world

The story of Mama Tembo's herd is the story of all African elephants. These huge land mammals are struggling to exist in a natural habitat that is rapidly shrinking. As the population of Africa increases and more and more land is taken over by people, there is less room for elephants. Many concerned people around the world wonder what the future holds for these breathtaking beasts and what can be done to save them from becoming extinct.

(right) This is Mama Tembo. Her name means Mother Elephant in Swahili, the language spoken in eastern Africa.

Elephant families

Elephant herds are made up of five to fifteen members. The fifteen members of Mama Tembo's herd are all related. Most are female elephants called cows. Mothers, sisters, daughters, aunts, and nieces all travel together. There are a few sons and nephews but, like all male elephants, these young bulls will leave the family and go off to live on their own when they grow up.

Happy together

Why elephants live together is somewhat puzzling. Most animals that stay in groups do so for protection but, because of their enormous size, elephants have little to fear from other animals. In fact, living in groups may even cause elephants extra problems. These huge animals need a great deal of food, and often there is not enough vegetation in one area for all the members of a herd. Elephants probably stay together simply because they enjoy one another's company.

Elephants care deeply about one another. They take very good care of their calves and lovingly tend sick family members. When a family member dies, the relatives of the dead beast stay close by and stroke the body with their trunks. Elephants have also been known to visit the remains of long-dead relatives.

Old and wise

The leader of an elephant herd is always one of the old and wise members. Mama Tembo is close to fifty years of age. She is a valued member of the herd because she possesses important knowledge such as where to find traditional water holes. As she nears the end of her life, she passes on her knowledge to the rest of the family.

(below) Mama Tembo's herd consists of her female relatives and their offspring.

(opposite) Sometimes related elephant herds meet up with one another and have reunions.

Elephant society

Elephant society is a complex network. As herds grow in size after the arrival of new calves, some of the animals leave to form new family units. The separation sometimes occurs when two dominant cows fight about who will be the leader. Different food preferences can also divide the animal group. When a new herd is formed, the members of the old and new group stay in contact. Related groups such as these are called bond groups. They are frequently found ranging near one another.

Family reunions

From time to time Mama Tembo's herd meets one of its bond groups. Like human families, elephant herds enjoy reunions with their relatives. When Mama Tembo sees her cousin, she greets her enthusiastically. She runs towards her, flapping her gigantic ears. Then she places the tip of her trunk into her cousin's mouth. The other animals run towards one another as well, trumpeting joyfully and entwining their trunks.

Clan get-togethers

Several bond groups make up a clan. Several clans that range in one area make up a subpopulation. An elephant population, in turn, consists of all the elephants in a larger area, such as an ecosystem or continent.

Clan meetings occur less often than bond meetings, but when a get-together does take place, the first order of the day is to set up a dominance hierarchy. The elephants rank themselves from strongest to weakest after a series of trumpeting and shoving matches has taken place.

During difficult times many clans may gather together for protection or because there are only a few places for them to get food and water. In the past these mammoth meetings sometimes included all the clans in an entire ecosystem, totaling thousands of elephants. Today it is rare to see more than several hundred elephants in one place at the same time.

Jumbo babies

Elephant pregnancies last twenty-two months. That's almost two years! When it is time to give birth, the mother-to-be finds a secluded spot. Inexperienced mothers do not know how to care for their first offspring, so they are often accompanied by a helper who assists them with the birth and teaches them what to do afterwards. Mama Tembo has helped many mothers look after their calves.

Welcome to the world!

When a baby elephant is born, it is covered with hair. Its mother lifts off the clinging birth sac that kept the baby safe inside the uterus. Although the baby weighs more than 250 pounds (115 kilograms) at birth, it is helpless. The mother and helper gently lift the newborn to its feet. Once standing, the calf begins to search for its mother's milk. Having found the nipples between her front legs, the baby nurses, sucking the milk with its mouth.

Elephant mothers are able to carry their babies until birth and feed their young from their own bodies because they are mammals. Mammal mothers have mammary glands, which produce milk for suckling babies. An elephant mother's milk contains nutrients that meet the particular needs of her calf.

Weaning the young

After a few weeks or months mammal babies start eating the same food as their parents do. The mothers introduce their babies to this food slowly. Gradually the young animals eat more and more solid food and drink less milk. The change from drinking milk to eating solid food is called weaning. Elephant calves start sampling the green vegetation when they are three months old, but their mothers chew the food first and place it into the mouths of the calves. The babies also continue to nurse until they are two years old. If a mother cannot nurse her calf, another cow nurses the baby instead.

Walking in Mother's shadow

Calves must stay close to their mothers at all times or suffer certain death. Predators have a good chance of killing a lone elephant under six years of age. For the first few months a calf seldom wanders more than a few steps from Mom. It often walks underneath her for protection. Mother elephants are very caring and protective of their young and look after them for ten years or more. They do not hesitate, however, to spank their offspring with their trunks if they get into too much mischief.

Baby elephants develop slowly and need time to learn their lessons, just as human babies do. Mother elephants teach their offspring what food to eat, which animals to avoid, and where to find food and water. The most difficult thing a calf has to master is the use of its trunk. At first, calves blow bubbles when they try to drink water. They must learn to suck up the water and then squirt it into their mouths.

Those tricky trunks

It takes several years before a young elephant has complete control of its trunk. More than just a long nose, the trunk is an essential tool of survival. It is the organ of smell and touch. The trunk enables elephants to drink and eat. The end of a trunk is quite sensitive, just as our fingertips are. This handy feeler allows the elephant to determine the shape, texture, and temperature of its surroundings. Trunks can carry very heavy objects, yet can be dainty as well. They can be used to lift a flower, tear down a large tree limb, suck or blow water, locate an enemy, fight a rival, or trumpet a warning call. These are just some of the things a young calf must learn to do with its trunk.

(opposite) At one time people mistakenly believed that elephant calves nursed with their trunks. In fact, they use their mouths.

(below) Newborn elephants walk under their mothers for shade, comfort, and protection.

Growing up

As each calf grows up, he or she develops a personality. Some youngsters are active and like to tease buffalo or charge lion cubs. Others are gentle and prefer to tenderly hold on to their mothers' tails with their trunks. As part of their training as future mothers, female calves around nine years old start looking after younger calves. Females mature between nine and eleven years, but the males do not mature until two years later. As soon as the young bulls start taking an interest in mating with the female elephants, the other family members consider them a nuisance and chase them away.

Young bulls

Bulls leave the family when they are about fourteen years old. When a young bull is forced to leave the herd, he stays nearby for a while but eventually leaves and forms bonds with other males his age. Adult bulls may be seen wandering by themselves or in small groups.

The mating cycle

Elephants do not have a fixed breeding season. They can mate at any time during the year, but it is not easy for bulls and fertile females to meet. Cows carry their babies for almost two years and then nurse them for about another two years. During this time they do not mate. That means a female is ready to mate for only a very short time once every four or five years. With so few chances to breed, it seems amazing that male and female elephants manage to produce offspring.

To make the situation even more difficult, bulls and cows are often far away from one another when the ideal mating conditions occur. How do the bulls and cows contact each other? It has recently been discovered that female elephants "sing" mating songs that bring bulls running from all directions. These mating songs are a series of calls that can be heard by elephants several miles away but not by humans.

(opposite, top) **This baby practices using its trunk.**
(opposite, bottom) **The calf runs briskly beside Mom.**

When bulls enter musth, as this one has, they often get into violent fights with one another. This bull lost his left tusk in a previous battle.

The period of musth

A major change occurs in bulls when they reach about thirty-five years of age. At this time a male first enters the condition of musth and becomes very eager to mate. Although he was capable of mating before this age, he is now a much more powerful rival to other bulls that want to mate with the same cow. In battles for a female, an elephant in musth is usually the winner.

Musth occurs once a year and lasts about three months. It is a difficult time for bulls. They seldom eat, and they use up a great deal of energy searching for and guarding cows. A bull in musth does not allow other males to approach a cow with which he wishes to mate. He can become quite violent, leading to serious fighting between him and a rival bull. During these fights bulls occasionally break their tusks and are even capable of killing each other.

Elephant facts

Size and speed

Elephants are the largest land animals in the world. An adult male elephant grows to an average height of eleven feet (three-and-a-half meters) and weighs 12,000 pounds (5,400 kilograms). A few African bulls weighed nearly double this amount. Female elephants are smaller, weighing about 10,000 pounds (4,500 kilograms) and reaching ten feet (three meters) in height.

Although elephants are big, bulky creatures, they can outrun human beings. An elephant walks at about the same speed as a person, but it can run up to twenty-four miles (thirty-eight kilometers) per hour for short distances. Elephants are so big, though, that they cannot jump.

Intelligent and affectionate

The elephant has the largest head and biggest brain of any land animal. Its higher intelligence makes it capable of passing on complex messages to other elephants. It is also an extremely social and affectionate creature. Elephants nuzzle one another when they say hello because they enjoy one another's company immensely.

Saggy, baggy skin

Elephant skin wrinkles and sags and looks as if it is several sizes too big. The skin is thick, but elephants still suffer badly from insect bites. They often roll in the mud to coat their skin, making it harder for insects to penetrate the surface. The deep creases on the lower part of an elephant's leg vary from elephant to elephant. Because these folds are unique, they can be used to identify the animals, just as fingerprints are used to identify human beings.

African elephant skin is so wrinkled that it looks two sizes too big.

Multi-purpose noses

Elephants have the longest noses of any creature in the world. Elephant trunks contain over forty thousand muscles and tendons. They can lift huge logs and small elephant calves. As well as being strong, trunks are flexible. They can bend, curl, lift, and grasp. The two flexible "fingers" at the end of the trunk are capable of picking up a single leaf or even a blade of grass. An elephant uses its trunk to suck up water and then squirt it down its throat. The trunk has nostrils at the end, so it is also used for breathing, smelling, and trumpeting.

Elephants have the longest noses in the world.

Knees and toes

The elephant is the only animal with four knees. Its front and back legs both bend in the same direction. When the elephant walks, its back feet land in exactly the same spot as its front feet did.

Although an elephant weighs several tons, it actually walks on its toes. An elephant has four big toes with a large pad underneath that acts as a cushion. The thick padding allows this huge animal to walk through the forest in graceful silence.

The special construction of elephant knees and toes enables elephants to walk both quietly and gracefully.

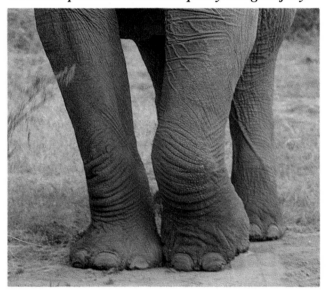

Life and death

Compared to most other animals, elephants have long lives. The life span of a wild elephant is fifty to sixty years. Elephants in captivity sometimes live until they are seventy years of age. During their lifetime elephants grow six sets of four teeth. Once the final set has worn down, the animals find it difficult to tear off branches—nor can they chew well enough. Lack of nourishment causes older elephants to grow weak and die. Elephants also die as a result of accidents such as getting stuck in mud or being struck by falling trees.

Elephant tusks are just overgrown teeth.

Staying cool

Elephants love to play in water. They take baths several times a day and use their trunks to squirt water at one another. Elephants also cool down by standing in the shade and flapping their enormous ears. An elephant's ears contain many blood vessels. When the elephant flaps its ears, the blood inside is cooled. As the cooled blood circulates throughout the body, it brings down the elephant's temperature.

Built-in snorkels

Despite their huge size, elephants are capable swimmers. They sometimes cross lakes and rivers by swimming with their bodies totally immersed underwater except for the tips of their trunks, which stick above the water like snorkels and allow the elephants to breathe as they swim along underneath.

Lopsided tusks

The tusks of an elephant are two incisors that have grown very large. Just as a person is left- or right-handed, an elephant is left- or right-tusked. The tusk the animal favors is always longer than the other. Tusks are used for digging, carrying, and as weapons. A baby elephant's first set of tusks is replaced when the calf is two years old.

In search of food and water

Mama Tembo and her family consume a lot of food to support their mammoth sizes. Adult elephants eat up to 300 pounds (135 kilograms) of food each day. Elephants eat leaves, bark, branches, and berries, and they wander over most of the African continent in search of these foods. Elephants range in the rain forests of the west coast, the desert-like areas of the north, and in the cooler regions of the south. Few other animals have such extensive feeding areas. When an elephant herd travels long distances, the animals walk in a line from largest to smallest, with the leader at the front.

(top) Mama Tembo tears off a branch to get at some tasty leaves. Elephants spend most of their day eating.

A long dry season

Mama Tembo's herd lives in a subtropical climate. The amount of precipitation in the area changes drastically from season to season. Sometimes months go by without any rain, followed by weeks of constant, heavy downpour. The animals must be able to adapt to the dry times and take advantage of the short wet periods. Some animals are able to get the moisture they need from the water stored in plants. Predators survive by drinking the blood of their prey. Most animals, however, must make long treks to the scattered water holes or dig for water in the riverbeds.

Good memories

From time to time droughts occur, forcing the herd to travel to faraway water holes or to search for hidden sources of water. During these difficult times, the elephant herd relies totally on Mama Tembo's memory. It may have been five or even ten years since the last drought, but the old elephant can still recall the location of distant water sources. Unlike the younger animals, she has trekked to these places several times during her long life.

In the dry season elephants also provide a helpful service to local wildlife. Their sense of smell is so good that they can detect water that is far away and even smell water that is below ground. Once they locate a source, they dig wells that bring the water to the surface, enabling others to benefit from it.

Changing the landscape

Because of their large appetites, elephants are like huge munching machines that can destroy their environment by eating it. In order to get at the leaves, they gouge strips of tree bark loose with their tusks, tear off branches, and even knock over trees. Once a clearing in a forest has been made, grass rapidly grows to fill in the gap. As a result, elephants are partially responsible for the huge areas of grassland in Africa. Too many elephants in a small area can soon change a forest into a desert.

Elephant reforesters

Elephants help replant the very forests they tear down. An elephant's body uses very little of the food it eats. Over half of the food, including many plant seeds, passes through the elephant's system without being digested. As the elephant moves from one part of its range to another, it leaves behind huge piles of droppings. These droppings are filled with plant seeds, which quickly take root and start to grow. In this way much of Africa's vegetation is constantly moved from one place to another, providing new food sources for animals.

Three ecosystems

The area in which Mama Tembo's family ranges belongs to three distinct ecosystems: the scrub forest, the grassland, and the rain forest. An ecosystem is a community made up of living and non-living parts. The non-living parts include the soil, rocks, water, gases in the air, and energy from the sun. These parts make up the physical environment.

The living community includes the vegetation and the insects, birds, and animals that inhabit the area. People, animals, and insects consume the plants that produce energy. Animals that eat only plants are called herbivores. Carnivores are animals that eat other animals. Decomposers are also part of the ecosystem. They are creatures, such as worms, bacteria, and fungi, that break down plants and dead animals into nutrients that are then returned to the environment. Nothing is wasted in an ecosystem that is left in its natural state.

In the dry season elephants can smell water that is below ground and dig wells to reach it.

15

Grazers and browsers of the scrub forest

The ecosystem in which Mama Tembo's herd spends most of its time is a large scrub forest. Although the scrub forest appears to be a dry region, there is plenty of vegetation. Short, stunted trees cover the area. Patches of dried grass grow around the trees.

Without a river nearby Mama Tembo and her herd could not live in the scrub forest. Although the river swells and shrinks throughout the year, it never dries up completely. Along its banks grows a thicker, richer forest. Here Mama Tembo finds enough food and water to meet the needs of her entire family.

Robbed of rain

The climate of the scrub forest is influenced by the nearby mountains and foothills. As moisture-laden clouds approach the higher land, the cold air here causes the clouds to cool and rain droplets to form. The rain falls in the mountains, preventing the clouds from reaching the scrub forest. Although the scrub forest does not receive much direct rainfall, streams run down from the mountains to the dry land or seep underground.

Plant adaptation

Ground water provides moisture to the long roots of gnarled trees. During dry times the ground water is too low for even these roots to reach, so the trees go to sleep. They stop growing and lose their leaves. Although they appear dead, they burst into life when it rains or when the ground-water level rises. Other plants store water in swollen roots. Since grass roots are short, the grass only grows briefly when it rains. Although it may dry out, the root systems remain alive, allowing the grass to sprout again and again.

There are two types of giraffes: the reticulated and the Masai giraffes. Reticulated giraffes, such as this one, have square spots and prefer the drier regions.

(above) Masai giraffes have irregular markings and prefer to live in damp regions such as the forests that are located beside rivers.

(right) While feeding, the gerenuk stands on its back legs to give it extra height.

Tall and small browsers

A variety of animals make the scrub forest their year-round home. Whereas elephants wander from one habitat to another, the resident browsers, which eat leaves and bark, stay put and rely on the small trees and shrubs of the scrub forest for their nourishment. The tallest browsers of the scrub forest are the giraffes. Elephants and giraffes both feed on trees. The giraffes are able to reach the top branches, and the elephants eat the shoots and the bark just underneath. The lowest branches of the scrub forest provide food for small deerlike animals called steinbok and dik-dik.

The gerenuk

The gerenuk, a kind of antelope, also lives in the scrub forest of East Africa. It prefers to eat the tender leaves of smaller trees. Looking like a cross between a giraffe and a gazelle, this long-necked browser can easily reach branches that are well out of the reach of most of its competition. This animal shares its browsing area with the rhinoceros, eland, and kudu.

(left) Grevy's zebra are found in the ecotone as well as the scrub forest. Unlike the common zebra, they never graze on the grassland.

Through the grasslands

Because the scrub forest cannot supply Mama Tembo's family with all the water and food it requires during the year, the elephants travel to the rain forest in the mountains from time to time. On their way, they must cross a broad area of grassland. Between the scrub forest and the grassland the trees blend in with the grasses. This area, in which two geographical regions overlap, is called an ecotone. It is richer than either ecosystem on its own because it contains the types of vegetation and animals found in both areas.

Herds of grazers

In the ecotone the elephants encounter browsers such as the black rhino and impala as well as grazers such as Grant's gazelle and the kongoni. As the elephants travel further away from the scrub forest, they meet big herds of wildebeest, zebra, and topi. Large gatherings of a single species are rare in forested areas, but they are common on the grasslands. Grasslands provide an abundance of one type of food, so there is enough for a huge herd. With little competition for food, the grassland animals are able to live in large groups. Forest-dwelling browsers, on the other hand, have a limited supply of food. Although there is more variety of forest plants, there is less vegetation available in one area. As a result, forest animals tend to live in smaller groups.

Predator groups

The herds of animals that live on the plains attract many predators, whose groups are also larger. For example, lion groups, or prides, are bigger on the grasslands than those found in the scrub forest. Leopards, cheetahs, and wild dogs also pose a threat to baby elephants and the other grazers. The hyenas act both as predators and scavengers. Their jaws are powerful enough to kill animals much larger than themselves. Yet, these hunters also feast on the leftovers of other predators.

(opposite, top) Two Grant's gazelle spar for a mate.

(below) The Cheetah is the fastest land animal and can run as fast as seventy miles (110 km) per hour.

The rain forest

Mama Tembo's family ventures into the rain forest on a special trek. The elephants are not looking for food this time but for the minerals they need to stay healthy. These minerals can be found in areas called salt licks, which are scattered throughout this rain forest. For generations elephants have obtained the minerals they needed from these natural deposits of exposed salt. By instinct the animals know to lick the deposits.

Layers of vegetation

The rain forest is a rich environment made up of thousands of species of trees and flowering plants. Creepers and woody vines cover the trunks of some trees. All these plants ensure a large supply of seeds, leaves, and fruit during the whole year. The many layers of vegetation feed and house different species of animals. The top layer of the rain forest is the canopy. For elephants the food in the canopy is out of reach.

Swingers and hunters

Way above Mama Tembo in the high canopy branches the white-and-black colobus monkey feeds on the plentiful leaves. This daredevil monkey grasps firmly onto branches and makes bold and amazing leaps. At times it appears to fly! Other monkeys below him eat different varieties of leaves. The Syke's monkey prefers bamboo shoots and the leaves found lower in the forest. Small predators such as the mongoose and the serval, a small spotted cat, share the middle layer. They hunt the birds and smaller animals found at each level of the forest. As they follow Mama Tembo's lead, the elephants are not bothered by all the creatures around them.

A meeting in the clearing

When the giant trees of the rain forest die and crash to the ground, clearings, called glades, are created. Because glades receive a lot of sunlight, lush grasses and shrubs grow there. Elephants feed mostly on these lower layers of small trees, palms, and bushes. While wandering through a glade, Mama Tembo meets a buffalo. Buffalo are fierce, dangerous creatures that sometimes charge elephants. The wise cow knows this and cautiously turns to face the large bull head on. Fortunately, Mama Tembo frightens him off.

The serval is a small wild cat that lives in the rain forest where it hunt birds and rodents.

(above) The lively Colobus monkey lives in the branches high up in the forest canopy.

(left) The rain forest is home to a wide variety of animals. From time to time elephants go there to find salt licks.

(below) The Syke's monkey makes its home in the foliage near the forest floor.

Studying elephants

Scientists are just beginning to understand the elephant and its world. Finding out about elephant society is difficult because elephants have such long lives, and it takes many years to gather information on one family or herd. Now that the elephant is in danger of disappearing, a great many scientists and concerned people have a keen interest in learning more about the gentle giants.

Identifying the subjects

The best way to study elephant behavior is to observe one group of elephants. Being able to tell the animals apart is important. Each elephant is photographed with its tusks and ears displayed. Just like fingerprints, these two features change little over the years, which makes it possible to identify the animals. Although tusks grow throughout the life of the animal, their general shape remains the same. Especially important are the shapes of an elephant's ears and the tears in them. Because no pair of tusks or ears is alike, the differences between animals are easy to spot once a person gets to know the individuals.

Recording information

Once the researchers are acquainted with their subjects, the real work begins. Each day they observe an individual or a group. Video cameras and note pads are used to keep track of the events. After a long time and a great deal of study, researchers are able to see patterns and understand more about how free-roaming elephants get along.

(below) An elephant can be identified by the shape of its tusks and the tears in its ears.

(above) Mama Tembo's herd moves on when they hear another herd in the distance.

Elephant communication

Observing elephants can be fascinating. Let's watch Mama Tembo's herd at a water hole. As we watch, the animals are busy drinking but then suddenly move off. Why do they leave? The answer is that they hear another group of elephants approaching, even though these animals are nowhere in sight. Some people used to believe that elephants could not hear very well. Scientists have only recently discovered through observations such as these that elephants have an acute sense of hearing.

When a zoology student visited some African elephants in a zoo, she felt strange vibrations, or rumblings. She decided to try and record these mysterious occurrences.

She discovered that these rumblings were actually sounds elephants made by fluttering and vibrating air through their nasal passages. People had never before recognized these vibrations as sounds because they are below the human range of hearing. After studying computer recordings of the elephant rumblings, the zoologist found that, even though these sounds could not be heard by people, they were actually very loud.

The zoologist and a team of researchers went to Africa and discovered that elephants make a wide variety of noises with different meanings. When an elephant rumbles, the sound can be heard more than four miles (six kilometers) away! When another elephant hears this sound, it freezes in its tracks to listen. These special sounds enable elephants to keep in constant contact with faraway elephants.

African and Asian elephants

There are only two types of elephants on earth today: African and Asian elephants. Asian elephants are found in India and other south-eastern Asian countries, whereas Africa is Mama Tembo's home.

Different features

Mama Tembo resembles an Asian elephant, but in some ways she is different. An Asian elephant is smaller, and its features are not quite the same as those of Mama Tembo's. Its ears are only about one third the size of African elephant ears. The female Asian elephant either has no tusks, or they are so small that they are hidden inside its mouth. The tusks of the African male are much larger than those of the Asian male. The trunk of the African elephant has distinct rings on it, whereas the trunk of the Asian elephant is covered with small wrinkles. The tips of the trunks are different, too. The African elephant has two fleshy "fingers" at the tip, but the Asian elephant has only one. The shape of the Asian elephant also differs from that of the African elephant. The Asian elephant has two distinct humps on its forehead. Mama Tembo has a flat forehead. There is a dip in the back of the African elephant, but the other has a smooth, rounded back. Despite all these differences, both types of elephants share the same anatomy and ancestors, and both are tall, heavy, and have long trunks.

After reading the above comparison, can you tell which elephant is which?

Elephant history

Scientists have traced elephant history back forty-five million years to find the elephant's oldest ancestor. This tiny ancient animal was called a Moeritherium, and it looked nothing like today's elephants. It was the size of a little pig and had tiny ears and tusks, but no trunk. Since then there have been about six hundred types of elephants with various trunks and tusks. Only the African and Asian elephants remain. The hyrax, which looks more like a rabbit than an elephant, is their sole relative. Scientists believe that the hyrax and the elephant are related because their teeth, toes, and skulls are similar.

(right) The tiny feet of the hyrax resemble the feet of elephants. They have four short toes on their front feet and three toes on their hind feet.

Elephant problems

Many people visit Africa to view its great variety of exotic wildlife. They go on safaris, which are long journeys into the wild. Most come to take pictures of the animals in their natural habitats, although there are a few who come to hunt. Sightseers and hunters alike are willing to pay large sums of money for the experience. Elephants are a major tourist attraction and, in many African nations, this type of tourism is an important source of income. Even though the elephant is admired by all and is an essential part of the economy, its future is not guaranteed.

Shrinking habitats

To help conserve wildlife, several national parks have been set up in Africa. Unfortunately, most African nations are poor, and their populations are growing rapidly. Many countries cannot afford such large wilderness areas for animals because the land is badly needed by humans for growing food. As agriculture expands, the habitats of wildife are chopped or burned down. Even when large chunks of land are set aside for animals, elephants still encounter many difficulties.

Stress on the environment

When elephants live in enclosed areas such as national parks, they can cause major damage to their habitat by overgrazing the limited areas of the reserves. Fences prevent them from traveling to their usual food spots, so elephants are forced to feed on the same forest over and over again. The stripped trees do not have time to grow again, so the forest soon turns into a grassland. While elephants do some good by transporting seeds and fertilizing the soil with their droppings, it is not always enough. The seeds elephants carry and deposit onto the open grasslands do not always take root.

Conflicts with farmers

When there is not enough food in the parks, elephants quickly learn to raid farmers' fields by night. A herd can easily destroy a whole year's crop in one night. To save their crops, farmers strike back, using weapons that wound and kill elephants. These battles result in angry and frightened elephants that can do even more damage to crops, people, and themselves.

As the elephants' ranges shrink, the routes to their traditional water holes are sometimes blocked off. When thirsty herds find their way blocked, they become desperate, and their conflicts with farmers grow worse. The farmers have asked their local governments to prevent the animals from ruining their fields, but the governments are also under pressure to maintain the tourist industry. If there are no elephants for visitors to see, tourists will not visit and bring in the much-needed money.

Culling the herd

Although the general population of elephants is suffering greatly, countries such as South Africa and Zimbabwe have increasing numbers of elephants. Some people believe that over-population leads to the destruction of the elephant's habitat, which leads to worse problems such as widespread starvation.

To keep elephant populations under control, these countries rely on culling, or the selective killing of animals. In remote corners of the parks, rangers round up a herd of elephants and kill every member of the group except for the young calves. The calves are sent to other reserves or zoos around the world. The meat and ivory of the slaughtered elephants are sold by the local inhabitants. Although some people disagree with this activity, others argue that only extra animals are killed, and the money received for the sale of the meat and ivory helps the people who live in the area.

(above) *Living on reserves limits the elephant's natural instinct to roam great distances. Because they must stay in the same area all the time, some herds are in danger of overgrazing their habitats.*

(below) *A knowledgeable old cow leads her hungry herd toward a farm. In their weakened condition the elephants appear half mad. Terrified farmers sometimes shoot the elephants to protect their crops.*

The ivory trade

For thousands of years people have admired the purity of elephant ivory. Raw ivory was carved into beautiful jewelry and ornaments that were highly treasured. Piano keys were also made from ivory. Ivory was precious because it was rare and difficult to get. It was obtained by collecting the tusks of dead elephants or elephants that had been hunted in small numbers.

An outrageous demand

Today the ivory trade is big business. Ivory is sold to craftspeople in the Far East who carve it into decorative ornaments. About thirty percent of these ornaments find their way to North America. Once there were millions of elephants in Africa. Now there are only about 625,000 left, and the overall population is dropping rapidly. The demand for ivory is costing the elephant its very existence.

Some ivory comes from elephants that have died naturally. Some comes from elephants that were culled. Elephant hunting is allowed in most countries but is limited to protect the animals. Governments allow only a certain number of elephants to be killed, and special permits are required. These laws, however, do not stop hunters who know that there is a lot of money to be made in the illegal ivory trade. Most ivory is obtained by poachers, people who kill animals unlawfully. The World Wildlife Fund reports that eighty percent of all ivory is taken from elephants that have been killed in this way. Once the ivory has been carved, there is no way to tell how it was obtained.

The big business of poaching

In the past, elephant hunting was difficult and dangerous. Today modern weapons make it a lot less difficult. Groups of poachers sometimes fly into the reserves by helicopter and surround entire herds, which they slaughter in less than one hour. Within two hours all the tusks have been hacked off, and the murderous thieves have vanished into the air. In many cases the ivory is sold to pay for Africa's ongoing wars. The ivory trade is no longer a business from which a few people profit: whole armies are being equipped with the funds earned from this slaughter.

Stopping the slaughter

Some experts suggest that the only fair way to obtain ivory is to allow elephants to age and produce large tusks. When the elephants die of old age, the ivory can then be collected from the carcasses. This system would work only if poaching could be controlled. Some countries have import restrictions on all raw ivory and ivory products. If more countries would ban ivory from entering their borders, there would be nowhere for poachers to sell their ivory. If no ban exists, people can still make a personal choice not to buy products made of ivory. Without consumer demand for carved ivory, there would be no profit in supplying it.

Worldwide action

Fortunately the alarm over the possible extinction of the elephant is forcing governments worldwide to take action against poachers. The United Nations has drawn up an international agreement to control the ivory trade by setting quotas, or limiting the number of tusks that may be taken and shipped. So far over 150 nations have signed this agreement.

Several international conservation groups hope to raise fifteen million dollars to help save these gentle giants. These organizations believe that, by funding reserves and parks in Africa's better-run countries and promoting anti-poaching policies, they can save about two hundred and fifty thousand elephants. A major plan to educate the public on the plight of elephants was also recently announced. If these actions are successful, the elephant may survive.

(above) After the tusks have been hacked off, the bulky carcasses of poached elephants are left behind by the hunters. When park rangers find the dead animals, they pour lye over them to help them decompose. On the other hand, all the parts of culled elephants, are put to use.

(right) Today the major source of ivory is elephant tusks. Other animals such as the walrus and hippopotamus also produce ivory. Will they also become endangered?

29

The future of the elephant

The future of Mama Tembo's family is still uncertain. These fifteen elephants live in Kenya, a country that is rich by African standards. The government is committed to saving its wildlife. For the most part, the habitats of the elephants have been set aside as national wildlife parks. But Kenya also has the highest population growth rate in the world and is surrounded by countries that are unstable. Poachers continue to raid the country's national parks, and the elephant population is still declining. Will Mama Tembo's family be unfortunate enough to cross the path of ruthless poachers?

No one knows what the future holds for Mama Tembo and other elephants. People young and old can help by not buying ivory carvings and persuading others not to buy them either. You and your classmates might want to raise money for elephant conservation groups and research. The World Wildlife Fund has a special chapter for elephants. It is called Elefund. Money sent to Elefund will help Mama Tembo's family and the rest of the elephants stay alive for some time to come. It is certainly a worthwhile project. After all, can you imagine a world without a single elephant?

Something to think about

- Even one small bracelet has cost an elephant its life. Elephant ivory is only taken from dead animals, and most die as a result of poaching.

- In the past, elephant tusks were taken from huge male elephants because they had the largest tusks. Today most are taken from females because there are fewer males left. Many of their babies die because they are unable to fend for themselves. Tusks are also taken from younger and younger elephants that have never had a chance to breed. The average tusk now comes from a six-year-old elephant. If tusks continue to be taken in this way, elephants will soon become extinct!

- Governments cannot stop poachers until people stop buying ivory.

- Only elephants should wear ivory.

Glossary

carnivore - A meat-eating animal

conservation - The act of protecting our natural resources, including animals, from being destroyed

culling - The selective killing of animals to keep them from destroying their habitat by overpopulating

decomposer - An organism such as a worm, fungus, or bacteria that reduces what it eats into nutrients, which are then returned to the environment

dominance hierarchy - The order, from strongest to weakest, in which some animals rank one another

drought - A prolonged period of dry weather; a lack of rain that causes the death of vegetation

ecosystem - An interdependent community of plants and animals and the surroundings in which they live

environment - The surroundings in which an animal or plant lives

extinct - Describing species that no longer exist

ground water - The water beneath the earth's surface that serves as a source for springs, wells, and plants with long roots

habitat - The area in which a plant or animal lives

herbivore - A plant-eating animal

herd - A group of wild animals that wanders together. An elephant herd has between 5 and 15 animals.

hyrax - A small, harelike animal that belongs to the same family of animals as the elephant does.

mammal - An animal that is warm-blooded, covered in hair, and has a backbone. A female mammal has mammary glands that produce milk.

mating - The breeding of a male and female of a species

nutrient - A substance that a living thing consumes to be healthy and strong

poacher - A person who kills wild animals unlawfully

predator - An animal that hunts and kills other animals for food

prey - An animal that is being hunted by a predator

reserve - An area set aside where animals can live in the wild

rain forest - An area of dense tropical vegetation that receives a generous amount of rainfall and in which many different species of animals live

range - The area of land where a species lives

range - To wander throughout one's territory

scavenger - An animal that feeds on the remains of animals that it did not hunt and kill

scrub forest - An area of land characterized by stunted trees and shrubs

society - The system of community life in which individuals form an association for their mutual benefit and protection

species - A distinct animal or plant group that shares similar characteristics and can produce offspring within its group

subtropical - Describing a climate or area that is almost as hot and humid as the tropics

uterus - The organ of a female mammal in which the young develop and are protected before birth

weaning - The process of changing the diet of a young mammal from milk to solid food

zoologist - A scientist who studies animals

Index

     1 2 3 4 5 6 7 8 9 WP Printed in the U.S.A. 9 8 7 6 5 4 3 2 1 0